Ireland on $10 a Day
(Plus Shipping and Handling)

Don Carmichael

Don Carmichael

PublishAmerica
Baltimore

© 2005 by Don Carmichael.

All rights reserved. No part of this book may be reproduced, stored in a retrieval system or transmitted in any form or by any means without the prior written permission of the publishers, except by a reviewer who may quote brief passages in a review to be printed in a newspaper, magazine or journal.

First printing

The names of individuals in this essay
have been changed to protect their privacy.

ISBN: 1-4137-7660-4
PUBLISHED BY
PUBLISHAMERICA, LLLP.
www.publishamerica.com
Baltimore

Printed in the United States of America

*This essay is lovingly dedicated to my wife, Michele;
our son, Benjamin; our daughter, Genevieve;
and not least, to the kind and gentle people of Ireland who warmly
welcomed this wayfaring stranger to their lovely island home.*

The writing of this essay was made infinitely easier by the use of the word processor at the Decatur Public Library. I thank the staff for their assistance. I also want to thank Bob Reed for his suggestions and help in editing and Phil Coyne for permission to use his poignant verse, "Remembrance." And thank you, Bob Fallstrom, for referring me to PublishAmerica. I attempted without success to locate the owner of the copyright of T. W. Rolleston's poem, "By the Fireside." I also was unable to locate the owner of the copyright of the traditional Irish folk song, "Paddy's Lament." I assume that these properties are public domain. However, if I have infringed any copyright I sincerely apologize and will correct this mistake.

Afoot and light-hearted I take to the open road,
Healthy, free, the world before me,
The long brown path before me leading wherever I choose.

—Walt Whitman
From *Leaves of Grass*

Ireland on $10 a Day
(Plus Shipping and Handling)
A travel essay and poetry by Don Carmichael

IN THE 1960S A POPULAR "HOW TO" travel book, *Europe on $5 a Day*, was stuffed in the hip pocket of every college kid making summer pilgrimage to the far side of the Atlantic Ocean. Today an updated inflation-adjusted edition, *Europe on $100 a Day*, is more likely to encourage the pond-hopping hippie of former days—now 50-something, beer bellied and balding—to spend yet another sedentary summer with Fido burying couch potato bones deep into the backyard hammock.

A hundred dollars a day may be travel on the cheap for Bill Gates or Donald Trump, but if it takes a baleful bite out of your vacation budget, keep reading! I have good news for you: as a modestly priced public service I offer this underachiever-friendly travel package tailored for you and your cash-challenged wallet. *Ireland on $10 a Day (Plus Shipping and Handling)** is no nonsense, in the foxhole, hands on, do-it-yourself vacation planner that fits as easily into your budget as it does the hip pocket of your patched and faded bell bottoms. That is, in the unlikely event *you* can still fit into them.

*Note of caution: to assuage my pitifully overworked 57-year-old conscience I will come clean and confess that the "*Plus Shipping and Handling*" subtitle is a loosey-goosey loophole surreptitiously sucking up any and all costs above our $10 a day working budget, not unlike that ominous black hole in space that sucks up everything in its way: gravity, time, infinity, mothers-in-law, telephone solicitors…. So unless you can steal aboard as a stowaway in steerage of a Dublin bound trans-Atlantic cargo steamer prepare to shell out big bucks just to get there and back.

Here's the good news: with an innocent tweaking of the accountant's ledger, expenses of travel can be sucked into the black hole of shipping and handling and then cosmologically catapulted into a pie-in-the-sky twilight zone of hefty tax write-offs never to be seen or heard from again. And with any luck at all you won't be seeing or hearing from the IRS either. However, in the Murphy's Law scenario that you do and polite chitchat takes a sharp turn south, don't take it personally. Stay positive and see it for what it is: an opportunity to meet people and entertain new friends Club Fed style. And with its restricted travel itinerary, you'll have the leisure to cool your heels while you take time to contemplate those mysterious black holes…. Enjoy! Having eased my conscience for the moment by establishing the integrity, however dicey, of our $10 a day budget, let's proceed.

I can't deny that some inflation has occurred over the past 40 years; I may not remember much about yesterday, but nevertheless I clearly remember back in the day when a bottle of pop cost a dime; when a kid could make a good living, even finance his baseball card collection by redeeming pop bottles for 2 cents each. Like everything else the cost of travel has also inflated. However, with my inflation-busting budget you will vacation on a mere pittance, chump change…

Excuse me while I condescend for a moment, but I have the unenviable task of explaining, without utilizing over-your-head differential equations, how I arrived at an affordably frugal $10 a day budget. In other words, I must keep it simple so that even *you* will understand. Impossible? Of course, but put on your thinking cap as I do the calculus: $10 a day is only a paltry 100% markup from the $5 a day of the 1960s edition, but a whopping 90% discount from $100 a day of the current publication. Get it? No? Once again; slower this time; pay attention: $5 inflated to $10 is a paltry 100% markup, while $100 deflated to $10 is a whopping 90% discount. OK, Einstein, now do you get it?

Having condescended to this level I might as well get in-your-face honest and talk to you like the mature, intelligent adult that is obviously above your pay grade: Don't get to entertaining any highbrow, top drawer touristy ideas; with my no frills vacation package you won't be pampered with bubble baths in fancy five-star hotels built into romantic Irish castles; you won't be pampered much with baths at all, maybe a sponge-off in the creek when the flies start to swarm.

And don't plan on forking over good Irish Euros to be a houseguest in any of the cozy "bed and breakfast" homes scattered throughout Ireland. Even those dirt-cheap youth hostels are beyond our $10 a day budget. (And thankfully so—who wants to bunk in a barracks full of a twenty-something crowd who, returning well lubricated from the pub in the wee hours and ready to rock and roll, crank-up Ozzie Osborne's greatest hits for everyone's listening pleasure? Not me!) Should you, however, decide that your travel itinerary is not complete without the hostel experience, don't be put off by the moniker "*youth*" in youth hostile. Proprietors, when the vacancy sign is hanging, tend to subscribe to a fairly generous definition of youth, meaning anyone under, say, 95 who has cash or plastic in hand.

To see Ireland on $10 a day you won't be traveling business class, tourist class, steerage class or even fugitive from justice class; you will travel as a hermit. You heard me right, a hermit! Specifically, a 12th-century medieval hermit just returned from the last Crusade, clad in the dapper fashion of that day: rotting tunic and bare feet. On second thought, forget the rotting tunic; they are just too difficult to find these days. This medieval leisure suit fell from grace several centuries back and hasn't made much of a fashion statement since. Even the local Salvation Army secondhand store rarely stocks them anymore, and when by chance one is hanging on their rack it is usually well hidden between those natty Nehru jackets.

As for bare feet, the stony paths of Ireland will try the patience of the most resolute and disciplined ascetic, provoking XXX-rated tirades not recommended for the family audience. In fine print of his 6th-century Rule for hermits, St. Benedict addressed this recurring issue noting the frequency and ferocity of these unbecoming verbal outbursts. In his amended Rule is the proviso: while on pilgrimage in Ireland, in concession to rugged terrain of jagged rocks ripping oh so tender footsies triggering pernicious and prolonged episodes of pilgrim potty mouth, sandals—Birkenstock for the well-heeled hermit—can be worn if so desired.

After a long day of pilgrimage and tired as a donkey from pulling his two-wheeled trolley—the donkey cart of former centuries sans the donkey—the hermit will retire to spartanly sumptuous accommodations of tent, sleeping bag and tin cup (for coffee; or when the coffee ration is exhausted, begging). This—the hermit's portable Holiday Inn—is packed conveniently on his donkey cart and waiting to be put to service. Nightie-night, donkey-dude.

Of course, the 12th-century medieval hermit's mode of travel is not rental car or oversized tourist bus stuffed with middle-aged, camera slinging Americans. The hermit travels Ireland one sandaled foot at a time, treading rutted, craggy paths through fields of sheep and cattle, always with a wary eye to avoid freshly downloaded pasture pies, while seeking a meadow to pitch his tent, preferably near a trout stream to spice his scant board of carrot a la carte.

When the modern hermit tires of extending one foot in front of the other pedestrian style, he can, according to St. Benedict's Rule, extend a happy camper thumbs-out to passing cars with the hope of traveling passenger style. Loosely translated from the original Latin, an obscure passage of the 6th-century Rule appears to give 21st-century over-the-road hermits permission to hitchhike. (Something akin to the loophole used by old-order Amish giving them thumbs-up to ride to town in their English neighbor's Hummer to do some shopping at Wal-Mart on a Saturday afternoon.)

Fortunately, hitching a lift in Ireland is not the same desperate arm-tiring exercise in futility as in the U.S. Extend your thumb in the Emerald Isle where cars are passing, and drivers stop. Really! The operative phrase here is "where cars are passing." On quiet back roads you will more likely be passed by country folk on bicycles with their sheep dogs tagging along behind. When this hermit began hitchhiking Ireland I spent hours pulling my donkey cart over rarely traveled country lanes, until this donkey wised up and kept to the main roads where there is auto traffic. I rarely spent more than five to ten minutes hitching a lift on these roads.

In Ireland, drivers, who, in this crime-conscious American's opinion, probably shouldn't stop, do stop: for instance, females traveling alone often stop to provide lifts to hitchhikers. Throwing my cart into the trunk and myself into the passenger seat, off we go; I being sorely tempted to lecture my female chauffeur on the danger of stopping to give strangers a lift. In County Mayo in the west of Ireland, an older couple kindly pulled over to give me a lift. I jumped into the back seat to find myself sitting beside their 4- or 5-year-old grandchild; biting my tongue as we cruised down the road toward the town of Westport.

The Irish are trusting. In the opinion of this typically untrusting Yankee, too trusting; way too trusting. Several times when entering a shop to purchase groceries I found that the proprietor was temporarily absent. Although open for business, no one was minding the store. I waited alone for the clerk to return. Another time the shopkeeper, apologizing as he excused himself, exited to run an errand down the street, leaving me alone to shop. In a fishing tackle store in Kells, County Meath, the clerk opened for my perusal a large tray containing thousands of expensive hand-tied flies. To my amazement he left the room, graciously, though to my American mind foolishly giving me the privacy and leisure to make selections for purchase or, for the less ethical hermit, opportunity to reduce his inventory the old-fashioned way. *Never in America*, I was thinking.

Hitchhiking south from the town of Cavan in County Cavan, I was given a lift by an Irish fellow dressed in street clothes and driving a civilian car. After conversing for a while he told me that he was an Irish police officer. When I asked if he carried a gun while on duty he told me that he did not; some officers choose to, some don't, he explained. Again I thought: *That's not the way it's done in my country.*

In another shop I waited, trying to be patient, as the clerk spent several minutes casually shooting the breeze with the customer ahead of me. Here in Ireland, where to some extent old-world values still exist, especially in rural towns and villages, life remains slower, no need for haste. But this is Ireland. The problem is not that the Irish are trusting or that they conduct business at their own pace. Trust is still a virtue in our world, isn't it? And just because we Americans seem always to rush doesn't mean Irish folk must hurry, does it? No, the problem is not that the Irish are trusting or are in no hurry to conduct their business. Maybe the problem is we Americans are too untrusting and too impatient to conduct our business.

Before leaving this subject, one more story to illustrate the character of the Irish people. I had hitched a ride into isolated countryside in the north of County Mayo, a few miles from the town of Foxford. I planned to pitch my tent and cast a fly to rising trout. The proprietor of a fishing tackle shop in Balina kindly directed me to a trout stream, a tributary of Ireland's famous salmon river, the Moy, where I would have the solitude I desired for camping and casting flies.

Hitching a lift to the vicinity of the stream I exited the car with my cart. In my haste, I unwittingly left, of all things, my fly rod in the back seat. Unaware of my mistake I pulled my cart along a lazy country lane bordered on either side by dry stone walls overgrown with ivy. Coming upon a picturesque meadow of grazing sheep, with an ancient stone bridge arching the stream, I had found an ideal setting this sunny afternoon to pitch my tent and spend a few days.

I began to search for the owner of the field by following the pleasant scent of burning peat to its source where I discovered a little whitewashed cottage nestled across the way. The field's owner was at home sitting next to a hearth fire. Introducing myself, I asked for permission to pitch a tent in the sheep pasture next to the stream.

"Of course," she replied. Then with a bit of hesitation I continued with the next request, could I camp for a week or so?

"Stay all summer if you've a mind," was her smiling reply, so typical of Irish hospitality.

Back to the AWOL fly rod. As I was pitching my tent, the driver who had given me a lift was returning to his home in Dublin on the other side of Ireland. However, discovering my fly rod in his back seat, he reversed direction and made the trip back just to return my fishing tackle. "You won't catch trout without this," he laughed, handing me the rod. This is why I love the Irish: so many unselfish acts of kindness and generosity were bestowed on this stranger, for no other reason than that's just the way Irish are.

The ocean, lakes and streams of Ireland provide for world-class salmon and trout fishing. I am a dry fly angler, but being from the Midwest most of my fly rod experience is on rivers and streams fishing for smallmouth bass. I know where and how to catch bass with a fly rod, but I don't claim to be an accomplished trout angler. I cast dry flies for stream trout and have caught some, mainly rainbows 10 to 12 inches. The largest trout I caught was an eighteen-inch brown in Utah's Provo River. Most of my fishing in Ireland was while wading in small streams; consequently the brown trout I caught were small, though plentiful in numbers. Also, while in Ireland I decided that I would spend my time hiking rather than fishing, the rationale being that I can fish anywhere, but I can only hike Ireland while in Ireland.

Anglers like to debate which species of fish provides the most sport, trout or smallmouth bass. Both are powerful fighters and inhabit similar stream environments, though their diets and eating habits are quite dissimilar: trout prefer the smallest insects and insect larva, while smallmouth prey on much larger fare. An immigrant introduced to American waters, the brown trout is European royalty, a fish with the classically refined appearance of a Pisces aristocrat. Elegantly attired in spotted dinner jacket, this trout sips insects from surface water with impeccable manners as though having tea with the queen of England. While this may be proper dining etiquette for old-world aristocracy, it just isn't the way a great sport fish ought to chow down. The smallmouth bass, by contrast, is a red-blooded American species and behaves like it: with crude frontier table manners this fish attacks a meal like a half-starved pit-bull terrier, coming out of the water to take what he wants and making such a commotion that a daydreaming angler will be instantly startled into reality....

The Poetry of Nature's Way

*Delicate reeds split from shoots of Calcutta cane
Mitered in tapered artistry become the bamboo fly rod,
Imperially slender, balanced, ever flexing,
The angler's Stradivarius
Casting ribbons of floating line
With finely crafted hand-tied flies:
Pastoral scenes of sylvan phantoms
Soaring over prairie streams
Under balmy summer skies
To ride the stony riffles
Then perch on silent pools
Where watching from his lair below
The hunter stalks his wing'ed foe...
Will fins rise to take the fly
Or refuse the tempter's lie (?)
When predator becomes the prey,
The poetry of nature's way.
With startling splash and flash of fins
The stalker strikes, the fight begins
When fly reel spins and bamboo bends
As fly line follows after fins.
Of a sudden breaking water
Bounding from his stony lair
Angry Pisces leaps through air
Shaking fast his lying foe
(Wounded pride's frenzied show)
Though stubborn snare won't let go.
In time fins tires, his strength expires
Comes sulking to the net but still not yet*

DON CARMICHAEL

A sportsman proved till snare removed
Fins swims away set free to fight another day.
With summer's end alas the angling sport shall pass
Though surely blest in winter's rest
The angler dreams of prairie streams,
Bamboo rods and hand-tied flies...
But a word to the wise:
Will caution reign before you rise
To finely crafted tempting lies (?)
When predator becomes the prey,
The poetry of nature's way.

PACKING HIS FLY ROD FOR THE moment on the donkey cart, this hermit continues his pilgrimage, not to some venerated shrine or to the ruins of an ancient church hidden in some remote glen. Rather, a pilgrimage of back roads, country lanes and hiking paths across the Emerald Isle, getting to know her people, and in the experience learning something of himself and his country.

The original journey, a month in the spring of 2003, was a memorable experience. When the following spring rolled around and the weather warmed, thawing my gypsy spirit, I decided to return. For a month in the summer of 2004 I resumed my pilgrimage, again pulling my donkey cart and traveling as a 12th-century medieval hermit through 21st-century Ireland. A married hermit on pilgrimage will travel no farther than the length of his wife's leash. This hermit's pilgrimage to Ireland was possible because I have been blessed with my lovely and loving wife Michele, and though she refused to hike Ireland with me in the fashion of a 12th-century hermit on a $10 a day budget, she selflessly extended the leash so that I could....

To Michele

The cost of love is dear, indeed,
Tendered with each tear,
Always paid in full
Each and every year;
But to our hearts there is no charge,
This love forever free...
Is this because the love we share
Was always meant to be?

BEFORE THIS PIPE DREAM, THERE WERE others: like the recurring dream of building a traditional Irish cottage in my back yard. My vision was not so much to build, but to plant a stone cottage, as one seeds and cultivates a garden to eventually blossom into a place of lovely rainbow flowers. I began by seeding my imagination, sowing in good soil pleasant thoughts of pastoral Irish cottages. In time these seeds would germinate, taking root and sending forth shoots, eventually coming to fruition as a simple peasant cottage with stone hearth and dirt floor, as natural and miraculous as ivy and morning glory vines climb its walls of stone. This garden cottage even included many generations of families, pious and humble tillers of soil, who through centuries, in spite of the turbulence of life—or *because* of the turbulence of life—made their homes, beneath its humble roof of thatch, a safe and secure little shelter of love to birth and rear children... This was the dream as seen through the reputedly crazed eyes of a self-proclaimed visionary, medieval hermit and *wannabe* 12th-century stonemason. Never underestimate the power of pipe dreams....

A Starry Night

A starry night to contemplate
What can or cannot be....
Do sloops of candles burning
Sail this wine-dark velvet sea....
Did candle tallow dripping
Become our galaxy....
Does the candle maker's candle
Light eternity....
A starry night to contemplate
What can or cannot be....

WITH FRUITION OF THE VISION, ENOUGH with pipe-dreaming, I decided to act. This convinced my neighbors (if they needed convincing) that I was crazy. My wife lives with me, she doesn't need convincing. However, to reassure Michele I explained that the garden cottage would be one of my gifts to her for our wedding anniversary in late summer. This brought her aboard ship; the neighbors, scratching their heads, watched from shore as I set sail to work. I tackled the job, hand selecting stones, mixing mortar and working evenings after my day job and on weekends. I was hoping to finish the cottage by our anniversary, not appreciating the scope of the project I bit off and then had to chew. I didn't meet the deadline. I finished two weeks into October; our 25th wedding anniversary was September 11, 2001. Yeah, 9-11-01, for my wife and me this day was, to borrow from Charles Dickens, the best of times and the worst of times.

Americans sometimes choose Ireland as their European vacation destination simply to avoid the language barrier of the continent. An episode while I was hitchhiking will illustrate the convenience of speaking the same language as the residents of the host country. Hitchhiking in County Kerry, I was given a lift by an Irish couple probably in their late 60s. The driver, a typically congenial Irishman, peppered me with questions about my homeland while telling me of his family, some of whom reside in the States. (As I came to suspect while traveling, seemingly 90% of Irish have family in America.)

The gentleman spoke, as many Irish do, with a heavy brogue; I often had to ask him to repeat himself. Perking my ears, I would listen closely, trying to catch a word here and there. After a while I was about to give up in frustration when the man's wife mercifully intervened as translator. So as we cruised along the winding coastal road, heading south toward the Ring of Kerry, the driver and I cordially chatted as his wife kindly translated her husband's English into my English so that we could converse in English. This is why Americans come to Ireland rather than, say, France or Germany—no language barrier here!

Unlike us humans who are dependent on language to communicate, Mother Nature never utters a word, yet provides for our needs. Her Laundromat was the streams I camped beside and the sun overhead. I had no complaints with the washing machines: streams in Ireland are paved with stones and crystal clear, ideal for washing clothes. The dryer, however, isn't so dependable, at least not in the west of Ireland where rain is scheduled every 15 minutes and is seldom tardy. On days when the sun showed her face only briefly and intermittently between showers, laundry can hang all day without drying. In her unspoken way our mother also teaches patience.

Camping near the village of Roundstone, I learned another of life's lessons. Searching the area, I couldn't find even the smallest brook to camp beside. Finally I pitched my tent in a field near a small cottage that appeared to be abandoned. On closer inspection, however, I found that the dwelling was home to an aging woman and her developmentally disabled adult daughter. I introduced myself and asked the women if they could direct me to a stream where I could wash a small bundle of laundry. The older woman told me that to her knowledge there were no streams in the area, and then she offered to wash my laundry. I accepted the lady's offer and later when she returned with my freshly laundered, ironed and neatly folded clothes I reached into my pocket for Euros. But she refused to be paid. No matter that I insisted, she adamantly refused the Euros. Later I tried to pay the daughter, but she also declined explaining that she and her mother washed my laundry not for money, but simply to help me. This family, living very modestly, surely could have used some extra Euros; however, their act of kindness was not for sale. Lesson learned! God bless them.

IRELAND ON $10 A DAY

While pitching my tent in a shepherd's field near Donegal town, a flock of sheep, apparently the neighborhood welcome wagon came to my tent to greet and meet their new pasture mate. Typical of sheep they were docile enough, at least during the day. The evening was another story: the setting sun ushered in a night of wild carousing and loud, guttural bleating just outside my tent.

The next morning the farmer, whose pasture I was camping, apologized for the night's commotion, having forgotten to remove the sheep from the field where I slept, or, more accurately, tried to sleep. I told him I assumed that last night was the boys' night out and was hoping that tonight these *ram*bunctious lambs, surely all tuckered out, would tuck in early. He laughed saying that they would cause me no more sleepless nights. Then he invited me to join him in watching his sheep dog herd the widely scattered sheep. This was a treat; the dog, a good shepherd, obeyed his master's every command, efficiently gathering these incorrigible party animals and coaxing them through the proverbial narrow gate to, I trust, reformed lives in pastures new. I asked the farmer how difficult it was to train the dog. He replied that sheep dogs instinctively take to it, no training required. I suspect that he was a bit modest about his role as trainer.

Early each morning I would leave my tent, camping gear and donkey cart in the pasture to spend the day hiking (and hitchhiking) County Donegal, the northernmost county in the Republic. One day I hitched a lift west to rugged high country stretching along the Atlantic coast. This region, called Slieve League, provides scenic though sometimes treacherous hiking. To help negotiate steep and craggy terrain I carried a stick as an extra "leg" to ensure footing and balance. For this purpose I brought to Ireland a finely crafted walking stick that I had found at a garage sale and purchased for a cheap rummage price.

Spending the day hiking, I was to discover in the oddest fashion just how physically taxing this activity could be to antiquated bones, *my antiquated bones*! In late afternoon after many hours of hoofing up and down mountain slopes, I began to hear squeaking, clearly audible squeaking apparently coming from my sandals and sounding like a rusty gate. Cheap shoes I assumed. When I listened more intently, however, I discovered that the squeaks were not from my sandals, but from my hip. My bones were squeaking like a rusty hinge on an old gate! The squeaky wheel gets the grease; in my case, a quart of calcium rich milk poured down the crankcase to lubricate those rusty bones. I would never presume to tell an auto mechanic or chiropractor how to do their jobs. However, with the first quart of milk the squeaking subsided, and with this simple daily maintenance my over-exercised bones remained squeaks free.

Bedraggled from tramping through Slieve League, I started hitchhiking the forty miles or so back to Donegal town. Given a lift to the small village of Kilcar, I decided to stop at a pub for rest and recuperation. As is customary in Irish pubs, the proprietor upon request kindly furnished gratis a cup of hot water for the coffee bag I carried in my rucksack. After a while, rested and ready to go, I hit the road and quickly hitch a ride. As we cruised along, I suddenly remembered that I had left my beloved walking stick in the pub. Oh well, too late now! You were a great friend, old stick. I spent many pleasant days in your company as we walked together through the Illinois prairie and here in Ireland. I want to believe that this was no accidental slip of memory, but that it was your destiny to return to the land of your fathers to spend your declining years in the hand of some old gray-beard, hiking the hills and vales of Ireland next to the Atlantic Ocean. At least I hope this is your fate, my good and faithful companion.

Later, in a shop in Roundstone, I was to replace that old stick and begin hiking anew with a pedigreed young pup Irish stick. Of course we will need to bond, and only with time does this happen, though we will surely become best of friends as we walk together through this wonderful world....

This Afternoon

A poet with his walking stick
Will see the world this afternoon,
Perhaps to saunter village lanes,
Perhaps to wander woodland paths....
No need for haste, this afternoon
Is time enough with time to spare
To see the world....
Then, perhaps,
To linger there.

The 12th-century medieval hermit is not a people person. He prefers his company in small numbers, preferably himself and his walking stick. However, on occasion he will tolerate a crowd, if only to observe human social behavior while enjoying a pint in his favorite pub. And certainly the Irish pub makes for a cozy place to kick back at a corner table next to the hearth, tip a pint, and do some people watching. As with every Irish hamlet, no matter how small, the fishing village of Roundstone on the Atlantic coast of County Galway has a pub or two or three. Here the modern-day hermit can settle in to rest his weary feet, nurse a pint of Guinness and observe as 21st-century fishermen and farmers gather on a Saturday afternoon.

Roundstone is down the road from the larger town of Clifton and sets at the bottom of scenic hills that slope to the sea. The fishing village ebbs and flows while hugging the waterfront; there are no straight lines in Ireland. The business district meanders down the main thoroughfare with its storefronts facing the ocean; each shop painted in a bright and happy tint is one, two or three stories tall, and different in color, height and width from adjoining shops—giving the village an informal, irregular and inviting personality much like Irish themselves.

There are no words in the English language to adequately describe the people of the Emerald Isle. Suffice to say they are ultra-gregarious folk who love to have fun. Over time, the public house has evolved as a unique community institution to accommodate fun, showcasing patrons' talents as poets and minstrels. With personality, charisma and their never-failing gift of gab, the Irish are natural entertainers with lively conversation, quick wit and happy music. House musical instruments—acoustic guitars, fiddles, accordions, tin whistles, whatever—never lay quiet long as rowdy conversation and raucous music create rollicking good cheer. Evidence (if any is needed) that the Irish pub's reputation as a meeting place for lots of blarney, good times and fun music remains solidly intact.

By sundown (10:30 to 11:00 p.m. in the summer in this island set high in the northern hemisphere) the pub's standing room only crowd has spilled into the street. No matter; the musicians continue to play, leading a grand if noisy sing along, with music and laughter resounding through the village. Space is cleared in front of the musicians as women and children take turns dancing the Irish jig to rhythmic clapping in this family-friendly atmosphere of village and country folk letting their hair down on Saturday night.

Getting his fill of the pub scene, at least for a time, the solitary, nature-loving hermit has plenty of opportunity and space in Ireland to avoid crowds and lose himself in lush pastoral settings reminiscent of those idealized 18th- and 19th-century English nature paintings. Except for the large city of Dublin and the medium size cities of Galway, Cork and Limerick, the Republic of Ireland is—even at the beginning of this 21st century—a sparsely populated pastoral island of hamlets nestled along streams and fishing villages which grace a rugged, picturesque coast.

To give the reader some sense of the geography, population and pastoral beauty of the Emerald Isle consider this: England and Ireland, island countries, are each about the geographical size of West Virginia. However, England has a population of around 65 million people crammed, especially in the industrial cities of the north, like sardines in a can; Ireland, with little industry, is home to around 4 million people. Of this, fully a third of the country's population resides in Dublin, with the remainder in towns and villages or scattered across rolling hills and rugged mountains; a verdant land of grazing sheep and cattle in postage stamp pastures, bordered by ancient quilt-work of dry stone walls with whitewashed cottages strewn like pearls glistening in the sun.

I, like many people from around the world, travel to Ireland for various reasons, not the least to walk. The island was seemingly created for walking. Leaving behind my pitched tent with camping gear and donkey cart (confident they will be here when I return at sunset), I throw a rucksack over my shoulder packed with a piece of Irish brown bread, a carrot and an apple and spend the day hiking. I pass humble thatched cottages sporting brightly painted doors and rainbow gardens, countrywomen hanging laundry in summer sunshine and old men pedaling bicycles along quiet lanes. From remote cottage hearths, low and gentle flames of burning peat-turf send bluish smoke curling above chimneys to perfume the countryside with its sweet, delicious aroma.

A spry old gentleman pedaling in my direction stops to chat; I tell him of my interest in traditional Irish stone cottages so common in the countryside. He tells me that his parents reared 10 children in a one room, whitewashed cottage with dirt floor and thatched roof; this was typical in rural Ireland in the early years of the 20th century. The family, he explains, resided nearest the hearth, while on the opposite side with no wall of separation the livestock were kept, the animals' body heat providing the cottage with additional warmth. After conversing for a while we shake hands and go our separate ways. As I continue my hike, I inhale the scent of peat lingering in the air and consider how blessed I am to walk this land and chat with these lovely people.

Ireland, especially the west of Ireland, is wet and cool, raining every fifteen minutes on the coast, every twenty minutes inland. OK, maybe I exaggerate a little, but not much; many nights as I slept rain kept steady rhythm on my tent. Several times while hitchhiking I was caught in heavy downpours and strong wind, getting soaked to the bone even while wearing rain gear. Climate wise, Ireland in spring and summer is usually cool, seldom warm, never hot, and generally rainy. This is an island, but it's not Hawaii! It didn't take this rocket scientist long to figure why the fields of Ireland are such a lush, verdant green: with rain falling every fifteen minutes and each field covered with cloven-hoofed fertilizer factories fast at work munching grass and depositing recycled turf builder how could the Emerald Isle be anything but emerald?

While camping near Foxford, County Mayo, I spent twenty-four hours in my tent reading and sleeping as rain pelted down. But at least I was in a tent, cooped though I was in a narrow one-person shelter—the better to retain my body heat, keeping me reasonably warm and bone dry through some very cool, rainy and windy nights. Once, pulling my donkey cart on a less traveled country road between Balina and Ballinrobe in County Mayo, I was caught in a rainstorm rivaling the Old Testament flood in Genesis. My original destination was Balina but when the deluge came I was soaked. Not caring which way I went, just wanted to get out of the weather, I extended my thumb in whatever direction car or ark was traveling when Noah and his crew, bless their hearts, took pity and stopped to offer a lift to Ballinrobe. That'll work, thank you!

In the mountains of Connemara I camped for a few days in the tiny hamlet of Leenane on the shore of Ireland's only fjord, Killary, spending my time hiking and fishing. Unbeknownst to me, one enticing stream I fished was the private preserve of a fishing club. With swift riffles and deep pools this was an ideal home for big brown trout, irresistibly beckoning this angler as I quickly tied a dry fly to tippet and began casting. Suddenly a loud commanding voice scaring the stuffing out of me came from behind: "Go! Go! Go!" Garda—an Irish police officer—barked, as he shooed me away. I quickly reeled in my line and hurried off, not wanting to further ruffle his feathers, provoking a fine, or possibly worse....

Continuing my hike through the high country of Connemara, I followed a brook to an isolated cottage set amidst pine trees. An old man was standing in the door. I waved and he waved back smiling; I took this as an invitation to chat. Introducing myself, I offered my poetry; he read the verse and mentioned that he too was a poet (no surprise, living as he did, alone and well off the beaten path, I suspected that he was either a hermit or an artist of some kind). Then he told me his story: His name is Phil Coyne, and he was born and grew up near Leenane in the mountains of Connemara, not far from his present home. While a young man of 21 he immigrated to the U.S. and became a stevedore on the docks of New York City. Eventually retiring after many years of service he returned to his native Ireland; just two weeks after he returned, America was attacked by the 9/11 terrorists. Mr. Coyne's boyhood friend, a fellow Irishman who had also immigrated to the U.S. and worked as a fireman in New York, was killed in the attack. During Christmas season, 2001, Mr. Coyne wrote verse to commemorate his dear friend and his beloved New York. He invited me into his cottage to read the poem....

Remembrance
by Phil Coyne

As we all come together upon this Christmas Day
Let's flash back for a moment to a place so far away.
Down from the skies above them there came a deadly sound.
Three thousand died that morning, most never to be found.

As we gather here this morning, a silent prayer to say
For God to grant them rest in peace, upon this Christmas Day.
Let's not forget the heroes, the ones who rushed inside;
Never to be seen again as hundreds of them died.

The friends they left behind them; the ones they loved so dear
That God will grant them peace of mind this holy time of year.
Heartbroken, they remember someone who should be there.
While by the dinner table there stands an empty chair.

Let's think of them this morning and say a silent prayer.
One moment they were here on earth, the next they were not there.
Our world it has been shattered by the deeds of evil men
But from those burning embers New York will rise again.

WESTPORT, COUNTY MAYO, IS A BUSTLING community and like many Irish villages a river runs through it. Crowded shops, restaurants and pubs stretch along either side of an attractive tree-shaded boulevard where quietly flows the River Carrowbeg. I spent several evenings hanging with locals in pubs fronting the river, discussing just about everything including the weather while listening to traditional music.

It should be fairly obvious to anyone reasonably knowledgeable of the various genres of American folk music that traditional Irish acoustic music, an emigrant to our shores, became the grand-pappy of our "hillbilly" Appalachian mountain music and, later, blue grass music, though losing its Irish brogue while picking up a Southern drawl. The musical influence, however, has immigrated in both directions as the traditional Irish musicians' repertoire includes a large folio of American country and western music. In Donegal town I frittered away a rainy afternoon listening to guitar, accordion and fiddle players—pub regulars using house instruments to perform Irish traditional and American country and western songs from the 1950s. These musicians took requests, playing the songs of Hank Williams, Roy Acuff, Ernest Tubb, Tex Ritter and Johnny Cash and any other tunes I could remember. Also, I once spent an evening at a loft club above a pub in Dublin listening to a jazz quartet featuring a tenor saxophonist, all native Dubliners, playing in world-class fashion the American born music of John Coltrane. Musically, and in other ways, Ireland is reminiscent of the United States during the 1950s.

Near Westport and in the shadow of the Croagh Patrick—the

mountain where St Patrick fasted for 40 days in 441 A.D.—I pitched my tent in the field of a German woman. Later I was to learn that she had emigrated from Germany to live alone in the Irish countryside, devoting her life to environmental concerns. Through a Republic of Ireland government program, something similar to "homesteading" in 19th-century America, she was given a traditional Irish cottage in dire need of rehabilitation and a small field. Her responsibility was to repair, maintain and reside in the cottage. Working alone, this woman dug heaps of manure from the cottage that had previously been utilized to shelter animals; in time she was able to move into the cottage, choosing to reside without electricity or plumbing. She heated and cooked at the hearth and carried water from a spring. She kept geese, chickens and horses while cultivating a vegetable garden and maintaining a small fruit orchard; living in harmony with the environment, while actively participating in organizations dedicated to the earth's environmental health.

One rainy morning this kind lady invited me to her cottage for tea. Peat-turf burned in the kitchen hearth to heat tea and warm chilly air as she shared with me her experiences as an adolescent growing up during the war years in Germany. Because of severe shortages, she learned to live without material things, and even after the war she continued her simple life, without modern conveniences. Eventually she immigrated to Ireland where she prefers a life of solitude in a rural setting. I suggested to her that she would appreciate the 19th-century writer Henry David Thoreau, a kindred hermit spirit and American prophet who loved nature and was devoted to a life of simplicity. She made note of *Walden* as a book to find at the Westport library.

In the village of Dingle, on the Dingle peninsula in County Kerry of southwest Ireland, I met another German woman—a twenty-something on holiday. She, her German boyfriend and I spent an evening in a pub listening to traditional music and talking. She was a social worker in Germany, so we had something in common. She told me that as a 19-year-old she had resided in Israel for a year volunteering through a German sponsored program to work with Israeli schoolchildren. This of course was commendable, but I was curious, "Why?"

"Guilt!" she said.

"Guilt about what?" I enquired, though presuming the answer.

"The Holocaust," she replied.

"But you weren't even born when that happened; you have nothing to feel guilty about!" I clumsily tried to assure her.

"Guilt...!" she repeated softly.

The conversation with the German gal brought to mind a chat I had with an Arab who stopped to give me a lift. I can't recall where he, his wife and their children had emigrated from, possibly Palestine. I do recall him telling me he was Muslim. The following year I was given a lift to Galway by a thirty- or forty-something husband and wife on holiday from Israel. The husband, who grew up in Russia untrained in his Jewish heritage, considered himself an atheist; the wife, born in Tel Aviv, told me she was brought up in and observes her Orthodox faith.

The reason I mention these kind folk with their varied backgrounds is as an excuse to wax philosophic for a moment. It seems that individually most of us—we siblings in our always fascinating though generally dysfunctional human family—sincerely want to get along, to live together in this world in peace and harmony; and usually we do, at least one on one. It is when we start hanging together in groups that our less attractive tribal instincts surface and we begin to cause trouble, both for ourselves and for other people. Or maybe even one on one, as Adam and Eve discovered (with a little help from a serpent "friend"), we don't seem to get along so well either! Oh well, just a passing thought while gazing into the kaleidoscope of life....

The Eyes of Man

Gaze into the eyes of man....
Journey to that mystic land—
Sail that sea,
Search that shore,
Sleep the night on moonlit sand—
Gaze into the eyes of man....

LIKE RELIGION AND POLITICS, PERSONAL HYGIENE is a sensitive topic to be approached gingerly, if at all, much like the 12th-century hygiene-challenged medieval hermit approaches bath water. However, in Ireland even the water-shy hermit will have difficulty finding a legitimate excuse not to bathe. Ask in the Emerald Isle for a hot shower and you shall receive. Several times when a rendezvous with bath water loomed in my future, I was provided shower facilities gratis in village hotels. While camping in a sheep field in Donegal town the landowner offered me the use of the family bathroom in his home. I also showered free of charge at a hostel in Kells (should the spirit move him, a hermit can shower at hostels if not for free, at least for a pittance—a Euro or two). Of course, Mother Nature's "public bath"—the stream I pitch my tent beside—is always available. I resorted to sponge baths in mornings; though a hermit suspicious of hot bath water is not likely to entertain the idea of immersing more than his big toe in the cold stream water of Ireland, especially on typically cool and windy days.

While camping near the village of Foxford, I hiked into town stopping at the first bed and breakfast home I came upon hoping to finagle a free bath. The proprietor, a lady maybe 10 years my senior, answered the door. I handed her a copy of my poetry. She read the offering, and then began reciting from memory her favorite Irish verse. Obviously she was a lover of poetry, especially Irish poetry, so I reached into my rucksack and pulled out a very old anthology of Irish verse published in London in 1856, only a few years after the potato famine. I had found the book in a junk shop somewhere in Wisconsin. A lover of old books, she delicately turned the time-stained, yellowed pages, then unexpectedly I was hustled into her cottage; the next thing I knew I was sitting at the kitchen table, sipping tea and discussing poetry with her. She interspersed our conversation with recitals of verse she had put to memory as a schoolgirl, pausing in her recitation to exclaim shame that children in Ireland are no longer required to memorize poetry as she was. Her knowledge of rhyme was considerable, as she paged through my book, pointing to verse that she had read as a child. By the time we finished tea we had struck a sweet deal: I would lend to her this old volume for the duration of my stay near Foxford and she would allow me to use her B&B shower.

While on the topic of poetry, this may be the appropriate place to insert a lovely 19th-century poem by the highly esteemed Irish poet, T. W. Rolleston. To my mind and in the far more authoritative opinion of my B&B friend, Rolleston's verse captures the essence of Ireland and her people (certainly much better than I will do in this essay)....

In Irish: Cois na Teineadh
(By the Fireside)
by T. W. Rolleston

Where glows the Irish hearth with peat
   There lives a subtle spell—
The faint blue smoke, the gentle heat,
   The moorland odours tell.

Of white roads winding by the edge
   Of bare, untamed land,
Where dry stone wall or ragged hedge
   Runs wide on either hand.

To cottage lights that lure you in
   From rainy Western skies;
And by the friendly folk within
   Of simple talk and wise,

And tales of magic, love or arms
   From days when princes met
To listen to the lay that charms
   The Connacht peasant yet,

There honour shines through passions dire,
   There beauty blends with mirth—
Wild hearts, ye never did aspire
   Wholly for things of earth!

IRELAND ON $10 A DAY

Cold, cold this thousand years—yet still
On many a time-stained page
Your pride, your truth, your dauntless will,
Burn on from age to age.

And still around the fires of peat
Live on the ancient days;
There still do living lips repeat
The old and deathless lays.

And when the wavering wreaths ascend
Blue in the evening air,
The soul of Ireland seems to bend
Above her children there.

A RETIRED IRISH BUSINESSMAN WHO, AS a hobby, breeds show horses on his farm near Kells, County Meath, allowed me to pitch my tent beside a stream that runs through his fields. After several days of hiking the area and casting dry flies to rising trout, I was packing my gear to move on when he invited me to join his family for breakfast. Later, he would kindly offer to drive me to a road where I could hitchhike. This saved pulling my cart several miles and was much appreciated. But for the moment as we ate breakfast in his dining room, I listened as this entrepreneur told with obvious national pride of Ireland's recent economic miracle. With the transfer to the Euro currency igniting an influx of European Union investment capital, the Republic of Ireland has become—he proclaimed quoting from an Irish business journal—the 11th strongest economy in the world. Ireland, he informed me, also has highest rate of home ownership in Europe. (This did not greatly surprise me; while traveling the island I saw housing construction everywhere.) This amazing economic growth in only a couple of decades is the reason, my friend suggested, for Ireland's new nickname: "The Celtic tiger."

After a long history as an impoverished island, times are finally good for the people of the Republic. Only a few decades back, he explained, the youth of Ireland would have to go to England or the U.S. to find work. Today there are plenty of jobs in Ireland and a growing national affluence. Even kids from the continent who travel in Ireland can finance their stay by taking menial jobs that go unfilled by Irish workers. As citizens of European Union nations these kids can come and go as they please and hold jobs in Ireland without needing work permits.

I mentioned to him that while traveling through towns and villages of Ireland, I saw no impoverished areas. The people appear to be adequately provided for materially. As a retired career social worker for abused and neglected children, I developed an eye for recognizing subtle and not so subtle behaviors and attitudes of children who are ill-treated. Young people in Ireland appear to be emotionally and physically happy and healthy. I frequently saw families spending time together, moms and dads with their kids, in parks, in shops, in churches…. Irish children are delightful with their rosy cheeks and sunny dispositions; they are polite and respectful, obviously well parented and a pleasure to be around.

While hitchhiking from Roundstone to the port town of Roossaveel, County Galway, I was given a lift by a woman, English by birth, who had spent thirty years as a clinical psychologist and family therapist in Ireland. I mentioned to her my impression that children in Ireland appear to be well cared for. I was pleased that her professional opinion confirmed what I suspected: indeed Irish children are generally well reared and loved by parents who invest much time and resources in their little ones….

Childhood

Children chasing butterflies
Across the summer lawn
With sunny wings fluttering
Catching wind then gone....
Children chasing fireflies
Across the village green
With summer's fleeting twilight
Glowing, then not seen....

THOUGH IRISH PARENTS TRY TO PROVIDE for their children, history has not always been kind to the Irish family. At the beginning of the potato famine in the late 1840s the population of Ireland was 8 million. Even during the famine Britain confiscated food in Ireland to send to England to feed the English, thus leaving many Irish to die of starvation. Faced with an increasingly impoverished Ireland, Britain implemented workhouses where destitute Irish were literally worked to death. To avoid starvation or workhouses, many people emigrated to the U.S. causing Ireland's population to fall drastically. Today with four million people, Ireland's census is about half of the island's pre-potato famine population.

During and after the famine years many young people faced heartrending decisions: a life of poverty and oppression in Ireland or emigration to America, children and parents separated and most likely never to see each other again. Many young men set sail from Ireland in the 1860s presuming a better life in America only to meet a sad and ironic fate: military recruiters waited at port for immigrant ships to conscript male passengers into the Union Army. Traditional folk songs often say in a few simple words what historians in their thick volumes of facts and figures struggle to communicate. Is this because the composers of folk songs often *lived* the history as opposed to mere study from a distance? An Irish folk song, Paddy's Lament, addresses this poignant chapter of the Irish immigrant experience in haunting lyrics of a participant....

Paddy's Lament
(Traditional Irish Folk Song)

Well, it's by the hush me boys,
And that's to mind your noise,
And listen to poor Paddy's sad narration
I was by hunger stressed and in poverty distressed
So I took a thought I'd leave the Irish nation.

Well I sold me horse and cow, my little pigs and sow,
My father's farm of land I then departed,
And me sweetheart Bid Magee I'm afraid I'll never see
For I left her there that morning broken-hearted.

Well meself and a hundred more, to America sailed o'er
Our fortunes to be making we were thinking
When we got to Yankee land, they put guns into our hand,
Saying, 'Paddy, you must go and fight for Lincoln.'

General Meagher to us he said, 'If you get shot or lose your head
Every mother's son of youse will get a pension.'
Well in the war I lost me leg; all I've now's a wooden peg;
By my soul it is the truth to you I mention.

Well I think meself in luck, if I get fed on Indian buck
And old Ireland, is the country I delight in
To the devil I would day, 'God curse Americay'
For in truth I've had enough of their hard fighting.

IRELAND ON $10 A DAY

*Here ye boys, now take my advice
To America I'll have youse not be coming
There is nothing here but war
Where the murdering cannons roar
And I wish I was at home in dear old Dublin.*

Sons and Brothers

To staccato cadence of marching boots
Against the cobblestone
We sing a patriotic song
To soldiers leaving home....
To plodding dirge of horses' hooves
Through fields of rotting flesh
We stare in charnel silence
As caissons carry soldiers:
Sons and brothers coming home....

I VISITED THE SITE OF A famine era workhouse near Kells—People's Park is today a memorial to the poor who died and were buried on these grounds. Britain inflicted heinous abuse on the Irish people with Ireland being a convenient target of British imperialism partly because of the close proximity of the two islands. Land was confiscated from the Irish by Britain further impoverishing the people, creating a nomadic, gypsy-like, indigenous people who, without land, took permanently to the road, known today as Irish travelers.

Ninety-seven per cent of the citizens of the Republic of Ireland are Roman Catholic; the other three per cent represent every Protestant sect under the sun, ranging from the staid Church of Ireland to storefront Pentecostals and every denomination in between. However, unlike the ongoing sectarian/political strife in Northern Ireland, the religious sects in the Republic coexist in mutual respect and harmony.

During the 18th century the practice of Roman Catholicism in Ireland was forbidden by Britain; Irish priests who celebrated Mass were subject to execution. One casts a critical eye at Britain's intolerant behavior toward the Irish. However, we Americans do well to remember the United States' treatment of indigenous North American peoples and our nation's participation in the international slave trade during these same 18th and 19th centuries. Every nation of people, like every individual, is stained with fallen human nature....

Weeps the Rose

Monarch of the garden,
She sits in proud repose
As knights with prickly thorns
Protect their precious rose;
Maiden of the manor,
She strikes a modest pose
In her garden reaping
This lovely summer rose;
Cut flower of the vase,
Her sorrow to suppose
When scarlet petals wilt…
Then surely weeps the rose.

INDEED, THE IRISH POTATO FAMINE IS a sad truth of history. Today, however, this hermit saw no evidence of a current potato famine in Ireland. Quite the contrary, there seemed to be a bumper crop of potatoes, virtually every plate in every restaurant and pub was heaped with both mashed potatoes *and* baked potatoes—like grits for breakfast in southern states, you get them whether ordered or not. I'm not complaining, mind you. After all, I had the pleasure of turning those spuds with leg of lamb and mixed vegetables into a happy truth of history. I ate quite well that night, thank you! And I must assume by the anecdotal evidence of folks at tables around me, bellied-up to their own heaping plates, that they appeared to be well-fed also.

Fine Irish cuisine—hocus-pocus—now gastronomic history was not to be the end, but just the beginning—merely the hor d'oeuvres to whet my appetite for a smiley face future of pub food still to come. I was determined to put some meat, preferable mutton, on my meatless bones, and did my lip smacking best to do just that; taking bold advantage of daily specials that crossed this donkey's path. In pubs and restaurants throughout the Republic this gourmandizing hermit broke bread; trading his humble board of carrot a la carte for the uppity cuisine of salmon and crabmeat. Also gracing his platter with fish chowder, shepherd's pie, and every hermit's favorite, Irish stew with freshly baked brown bread spread generously with Irish butter; gut-busting victuals washed down with pints of creamy Guinness. Fireside dining in Irish pub tradition: the cozy ambiance of an ancient stone hearth to warm the body with burning peat as fiddle and accordion warm the soul with Celtic reels (it doesn't get any better this side of the great divide). Bon Appétit!

Now, reader, lest you judge me too harshly, remember that man (even a hermit, especially a hermit) can live without just about anything—karaoke bars, *The Jerry Springer Show*, a Cubs world series, Rush Limbaugh—just about anything! But man *cannot* live without food; and as Scripture teaches, even a hermit does not live by reduced priced, days' old grocery store bread alone. He has a God-given appetite, a natural hankering—call it lust if you must!—that demands to be fed now and again with a hot, home-cooked meal. So with hunger pangs in tow and rucksack over shoulder this 12th-century medieval hermit hustles off to a 21st-century Irish pub in hot pursuit of the daily special, to turn yet another anecdotal dining experience into one big fat check, to be picked up and paid of course, then conveniently deposited into the creative accountant's cosmological black hole of shipping and handling, never to be seen again! *Ireland on $10 a day*? Life is good!

Before I leave my much-beloved subject of Irish food and drink, a brief word about two of Ireland's finest: Guinness and Irish coffee. To appreciate the rich creamy taste of true Irish Guinness—and believe me you do want to experience the rich creamy taste of Guinness—you will have to travel to Ireland; Guinness will not travel to you, it's a homebody that refuses to budge beyond the shores of Ireland. Brewed in Dublin, true Guinness can only be consumed in Ireland. Although "Guinness" is distributed throughout the western world, with the short commute to England, not to mention the long journey to America, this brew is hopelessly fouled (ask any Englishman or American who has tasted the real McCoy in Ireland). But the good news is: a pint of Guinness is well worth the trip abroad; trust me on this one. As for Irish coffee, a cup of this percolated jove concoction spiced with a shot of Irish whiskey provides a "top o' the morning" start to a day of tramping the Emerald Isle.

After hitching to Roossaveel on the Atlantic coast, I traveled by boat to Inishmore, the largest of Ireland's Aran Islands. Nine miles long and three miles wide, Inishmore is located 40 minutes by ferry from the mainland. Once arrived, I pulled my donkey cart several miles into the interior, away from the ferry dock with its tourist shops. Satisfied that I was isolated as befitting a 12th-century hermit, I got permission from a farmer to camp in his field where a lovely panoramic view of the ocean awaited.

A unique culture has evolved on these islands over the centuries. A rough-hewn, hardscrabble people, men and women who literally created their own plots of arable land to grow vegetables by digging soil from crevices in limestone rocks and carrying seaweed from the Atlantic to use as compost. These folk, separated from the mainland with its modernizing influences, have managed to maintain their culture and Irish language while scratching a living from this island of stone. Parents on the mainland send their children to Inishmore for summer holiday to learn the Irish language and to be immersed in traditional culture.

The mother tongue of the Aran Islands is Irish, also called Gaelic; the native population speaks English haltingly, as a second language. While mainland Irish are gregarious, fun loving and outgoing, the Aran Irish appear to be serious people, not given to levity. My first impression was that they are an unsociable people; this, however, was dispelled by conversations I had with farmers that I met during my hikes. A more appropriate description, I think, is that they are by nature a shy, quiet people, who are friendly when approached, but are uncomfortable instigating conversation with strangers.

After chatting for a while with a cowherd in the hills, I mentioned to him what seemed to me to be a noticeable difference of demeanor and personality between mainland Irish and Aran Irish. The farmer smiled knowingly and agreed that indeed there is a big difference. I asked, "Why?"

He thought for a moment, then smiled again and said, "That's just the way it is."

His blunt and simple answer to a difficult question seemed to me to be typically Irish. These are not pretentious people trying to impress, nor are they given to self-aggrandizing displays of intellect; they are what they are—an honest, humble, *and* intelligent people, three traits not necessarily linked together, but in describing the

Irish, that's just the way it is.

Cattle are the predominant grazing animals on the Aran Islands. Like the mainland, dry stone walls were built to divide the fields of Inishmore into tiny pastures where farmers graze their small herds. While hiking one day, I stopped to watch a farmer as he was repairing a wall with limestone he had quarried from a nearby hill. As he worked he told me that as a child he learned the craft of building dry stone walls from his father. I watched as he struck pieces of rock with a hammer, breaking the limestone to fit snuggly into crevices. These interlocking pieces of stone, he explained, create a strong wall without the use of mortar. He told me that well over a thousand years ago Irish monks developed this method to construct their "bee hive" hermitages; today these huts remain standing and still do not leak rainwater.

Returning to my campsite after a long day of hiking, I notice a young couple—tourists I assume, spending holiday on the island. Walking hand-in-hand far ahead of me, they turn onto the footpath leading to my campsite. As they come near my tent, the couple begin to look furtively about, this and that way, as though to ensure that they are alone. I walk unnoticed in the hills above and behind them. *Much too wholesome to be criminals*, I reason as they pass my tent and continue toward the ocean. Then an old man's sudden epiphany: these two people are not casing my camping site with nefarious intent, but are young lovers seeking privacy; though surely the cool, stiff wind coming off the ocean this sunset would discourage amorous behavior—more thoughts of an old man. Two lovers in the flower of youth are not to be deterred by the elements; even a hermit remembers this. So with Atlantic surf breaking against limestone boulders, spraying its fury over the very edge of Europe, the couple disappears behind curtains of stone as this old man continues his hike, leaving two lovers to their privacy.

My last day in Inishmore was bright and sunny. In early afternoon I strolled lazily along the Atlantic shore, my reverie interrupted by the strange sight of a herd of a dozen cattle with one lone donkey in their company. Making their daily rounds, this blended family paused at a sandy beach to drink the water; I was surprised to see cattle drinking from the ocean (how does the saying go: you can lead a donkey to the sea, but only the cows will drink saltwater—or something to that effect).

Reclining on a couch of stone, I relax to watch the animals. Above me, a blue umbrella sky sports billowy cotton clouds; before me, a lovely summer day—captured on canvas, this seaside pastoral scene would surely hang in the Louvre alongside the landscape paintings of Renoir and Monet.

They say you can't make a silk purse out of a sow's ear, but I found my tailor-made diamond-in-the-rough hidden among bovine beauties—step-sisters in a cliché-riddled revisionist Cinderella story of an ugly duckling donkey who, wondering aimlessly through this ungrammatical, convoluted run-on sentence, caught my eye then stole my heart, not in spite of, but because she stuck out like, need I say, a sore thumb. She was a homely creature for sure, even for a beast that carries a burdensome reputation for homeliness. And she was a friendly—though shameless—flirt, snuggling close as I petted her neck. But with her sweet disposition, how could I resist? I continued courting her until she tore from my affection, leaving her slipper hoof-print in the turf to return to jealous step-kin as they sauntered toward their grazing pasture, soon disappearing into yet another convoluted run-on sentence.

Smitten by this brief encounter, I try to dismiss my feelings as a schoolboy crush, mere fleeting infatuation soon to be forgotten. I continue my walk, though not in the leisurely unburdened fashion as before—try as I do I just can't forget.... Something about those dolefully penetrating eyes and protruding ears, and that jawbone snout generously adorned with a pearly-white toothy smile... Suddenly my heart leaps as I spy cattle on a distant hillside; I search the herd and again my pulse quickens—in a field of grass my sweetie is doing lunch, salad with croutons.

Joyously I run to her, but she turns away, inexplicably casting her gaze elsewhere. I vie for her attention, sacrificing even my dignity, but with each clumsy attempt I am ignored; she coyly avoids eye contact. This is not just the centuries-old game of playing hard to get; I know when I'm being rebuffed, and I AM being rejected—*dumped*, in the barnyard vernacular of adolescent farm animals. I see another side of her just now; not the sweet, innocent personality which so captured my heart, but a cold, coquettishly catty dark side… Please indulge this lovesick jilted Romeo as he soliloquizes poetic, spilling his hurting hermit heart into, according to *Webster's Second Edition*, the archaic lexicon of King James English: This lass with sass is also alas a stubborn jackass! Admittedly, pretty rough language here, probably not suited for younger readers; but surely this is the gritty slice-of-life stuff of Shakespearian stage, and (if I can find an agent) soon to be parleyed into a blockbuster cinematic epic…or at least a made-for-TV mini-series.

Dreams of big Hollywood paydays aside, I simply have to accept that my feelings are unrequited. Left with only memories of what briefly was and what might have been, I walk forlornly into the sunset, consoled with the comfort of knowing that, even if not adapted to the big or small screen, we'll always have Inishmore. Here's looking at you, kid!

To ease the pain I left the Aran Islands with my donkey (ouch!!!) cart, taking a ferryboat to the mainland coastal village of Doolin. Burdened with the guilt of my straying heart, I would later hitchhike to Galway to purchase a piece of Ireland's world famous Waterford Crystal, a souvenir for my faithful wife back home and, I confess, a guilt offering.

On the ferryboat to Doolin a bright, cloudless sky provides passengers a fine view of the Cliffs of Moher, towering hills that fall precipitously into the Atlantic Ocean exposing sheer stone walls. This dramatic scene seems apt metaphor of the "Old World" coming to an end not in gradual decline, but crashing down as the Cliffs of Moher to submerge beneath a seemingly endless expanse of water; only to resurface somewhere out there in the vast Atlantic Ocean as the "New World." The United States of America: a welcoming home for the people of Ireland, Europe and eventually the world, with liberty and freedom to begin their lives anew in the next chapter of Western civilization. Even today this noble experiment—*this finely woven tapestry of ethnicities*—continues.…

from: The New Colossus
Emma Lazarus, 1903

Give me your tired, your poor,
Your huddled masses yearning to breathe free,
The wretched refuse of your teaming shore.
Send these, the homeless, tempest-tost to me,
I lift my lamp beside the golden door.

An American Family
(Ca 1903)

He stowed his dreams into a cardboard grip
And carried them aboard the immigrant ship;
When he left Odessa for a better life
He had a cardboard grip and a pregnant wife.
Liberty is the lady with the lamp in her hand
Who greets them in the harbor of the golden land;
But life wasn't easy in the melting pot,
Sweatshop bosses didn't pay a lot—
By day he sewed suits on Hester Street,
By night he played fiddle to a Yiddish beat.
Soon momma gave birth to her little one,
Poppa was sure proud of his first-born son;
The boy went to school and studied real hard,
Someday he'd own a business on the boulevard.
Today poppa looks back over many years,
The life he sees fills his eyes with tears—
He says, "God surely blessed the cardboard grip
That carried my dreams aboard the immigrant ship!"

DOOLIN, A TINY VILLAGE AND POPULAR tourist stop located on the west coast of Ireland in County Clare some 40 miles south of Galway. I returned to this village mainly to reacquaint with my friend Paul (at least I considered him a friend although I wasn't sure he would even remember me from last spring)....

Last year, pulling my cart to town—a few shops with a pub and grocery—I stopped at a used bookshop to enquire of the proprietor, an American expatriate, where I might camp. She provided directions to a small, weathered cottage a mile from town, home to a kindly old farmer who likely would allow me to camp in his field.

Following her directions, I pulled my cart to a dilapidated dog-eared of a cottage fitting her description. I knocked on the door, but with no answer I scouted around until I found an old man, at least as dilapidated and dog-eared as his cottage, tending cattle in a nearby field. I introduced myself and chatted with him before making my request. He told me his name was Paul and quizzed me about my pilgrimage, listening curiously as I told him of my journey through his country. Then he told me about himself. In the simple, modest fashion of country folk he informed me of his worldly wealth: a cottage and two small fields where he grazed his herd of twelve cattle. Not much, but enough, he assured me, to provide a living while keeping him only as busy as he cared to be.

He walked with me to an empty pasture across the lane, not far from a meandering stream. I told him I was planning to camp for a few days, using Doolin as a base to hike County Claire. This was fine with Paul, as he wouldn't be grazing the cattle in this field for a while. Then I asked permission to take his photograph. I watched as he mustered himself, arranging his collarless "peasant" shirt while slicking down unruly hair. Then straightening himself, he stood tall and dignified, formally if a bit rigid as he posed for the photo. As I took the snapshot, I couldn't help to think of Paul as an anachronism of history—the European peasant—replaced now in much of the world by modern, high-tech agri-business farmers. But at least for the time being remnant souls like Paul are still tilling the soil and tending their livestock in the age-old tradition of rural Ireland....

Returning to Doolin this summer to see my friend, I found Paul once again in the field behind his cottage tending his cattle. I was greeted with a warm welcome; he remembered me—I suppose it is not easy to forget a 12th-century medieval hermit on pilgrimage in 21st-century Ireland.

We talked at length. Things are changing in his little corner of the world; Paul pointed to houses scattered through the hills that have been built even since I was here last year. He told me that the Doolin "city council" re-zoned fields next to his for residential and commercial development. He received permission to address this council and even convinced the assembly to reverse their decision. But, as he admitted, this was only a temporary victory; ever-increasing tourism to Ireland's west coast is writing on the wall; the countryside surrounding Doolin is more profitable as development for tourism than as pastures for gazing cattle. Farmers, Paul reasoned, are the real problem. A lucrative offer from developers and they sell their fields, not wanting to remember or not caring that grazing land has provided a living and a heritage to generations of families.

I could see the sadness in Paul's eyes as he personally witnesses the power of money, with its dark shadow of greed to destroy the past while creating a new, not necessarily better future. The Irish poet Oliver Goldsmith addressed this ever-recurring issue in his extended verse, "The Deserted Village." This poetry is excellent reading as a fine description of country life in eighteenth-century pastoral Ireland and as a powerful testimony of changing economy on society and culture. Constant change is the nature of our world, nothing remains static, and the consequence of economic change can be profound. Goldsmith's poem provides wise insight relevant to every age and nation—including twenty-first century America....

Long-Forgotten Poetry

Beneath a humble roof of thatch,
Beside a hearth of burning coals
In solitude of winter's night
A hermit reads by candlelight
From ancient volume's gilded page
Words of inspiration,
Wisdom of the sage
Where long-forgotten poetry
Reside from age to age....

PAUL, OF COURSE, GAVE ME PERMISSION to pitch my tent in his field. And I did, though I was a bit apprehensive of the mainly European twenty-something tourists with some Americans mixed in who traveled by foot, often inebriated and rowdy, to reach pubs setting at either end of the lane that passed by my tent.

Every barrel has a few bad apples, and judging from the many apples strewn around my tent, the bad apples used the good apples in that barrel as cannon balls with my tent as the target. The good news: the bad apples, with proper rehabilitation, could make an honest living pitching major league baseball; also, nothing was stolen from my tent. The bad news: the tent was destroyed (bad news for me and a young Japanese woman I had promised the tent upon leaving Ireland). Drunken young tourists, I assumed. In 10 years they will remember the incident with shame, but for now as "good fun." I know because I was young once and have the guilty conscience to prove it.

This vandalism was, to my mind, an Act of God. How so? Last spring, while hiking and hitchhiking the picturesque County Kerry in the southwest of Ireland—the Dingle peninsula, the Ring of Kerry and the town of Killarney with its beautiful National Park and lakes—I met an Irish fellow in a café in the town of Dingle. I offered him a copy of my poetry; he left to read the verse and later returned to my table wanting to talk. I told him I was in Ireland on pilgrimage as a 12th-century medieval hermit. He listened without reaction, causing me to assume that he thought it not unusual to travel as a 12th-century hermit—already I liked his attitude and listened as he told me his very sad story.

He had recently returned from a monastery, Glenstal Abbey near Limerick, where he had gone to seek spiritual consolation after the death of his brother. He described to me his wonderful experience in this Benedictine monastery where the Fathers and Brothers, priests and monks, maintain a peaceful, reverent atmosphere for worship, prayer and meditation. The more he talked, the closer I listened, fascinated by his story. He ended abruptly by asking me if I would like to spend a few days working in the fields with the monks in a monastery environment.

"Of course," I blurted, caught up in the enthusiasm of the moment before I realized what I was saying.

"I'll call Father Patrick and arranged for your stay," he said, getting up to make the phone call.

"Wait a minute!" I protested. "I'm not Catholic and I'm not Irish!"

"No matter," he insisted. I watched nervously as he dialed the phone, biting my tongue rather than admit that I wasn't even a real hermit, that I was charlatan, a mere *wannabe*, and a fraud! In the presence of real monks in a real monastery I will be exposed for the phony I am! I will be *excommunicated*; no I won't, I'm not catholic. The Swiss Guard will arrest me as a Protestant spy, an agent of Martin Luther. I quickly put together an excuse to decline the invitation: My dog just came down with pneumonia and I have to fly back to the States this afternoon to take care of Fido. Sorry! Goodbye!

"It's arranged!" he told me, smiling as he hung up the phone. "Father Patrick will be awaiting your arrival to welcome a pilgrim hermit to Glenstal Abbey."

I swallowed hard and smiled weakly.

Arriving at the tiny hamlet of Moroe, County Limerick, ten or twelve miles east of the city of Limerick, I follow my friend's directions to find what I assume is the monastery entrance—a charming path that beckons this wayfarer even as it disappears, meandering into an enchanted woodland of gnarled oaks and stands of pine trees.

Pulling my cart, I follow the lane to pass cattle grazing in lush pastures; I pause occasionally to linger beside ponds alive with colorful water lilies and swans, virginal white, basking in the sun. Continuing the hike—but with no monastery in sight—I begin harboring dark suspicions that this gullible American has bent sent on a wild-goose chase as pay back for impersonating a 12th-century medieval hermit. Serves me right!

Amidst forest near the summit of a hill, I turn a corner and to my astonishment am greeted with the most incredible sight since St. John the Evangelist was given a sneak peek of New Jerusalem. In front of me stretch impregnable stone walls, massive turrets and watchtower, with the imposing arched and gated entrance of an ancient castle.

I stand before this commanding medieval edifice of stone, not believing my eyes—like a country boy's first glimpse at big city skyscrapers, I gawk in wonderment and disbelief. To twist the words of the astronaut: With one small step around the last bend, I suddenly leap through past centuries to reach the destination of my pilgrimage— this 12th-century medieval hermit has arrived!

Finally recovering from culture shock enough to muster some courage, I timidly pull my cart through opened timbered gates, knocking on the first door I come to, feeling more like a medieval door-to-door salesman than a hermit. A real life, honest-to-goodness monk wearing a tunic with hooded cowl comes to the door. I stammer nervously, not knowing proper decorum to address a servant of the Church as I ask to speak to Father Patrick.

In a moment a frail, elderly gentleman of small stature comes to the courtyard where I wait. He greets me warmly, introducing himself as Father Patrick and welcomes me to Glenstal Abbey. Suddenly I no longer feel like a fraud about to be exposed; I begin to be at ease. These folks are nice—very nice indeed, and not at all judgmental of this interloper. I have the feeling that this is the beginning of a wonderful experience. I am not disappointed, in the next few days I come to know Father and the other priests and monks of this Benedictine monastery as gracious and gentle servants of Christ.

After supping thin gruel from an earthen bowl, I am escorted by a monk in black hooded tunic to my sleeping quarters. Holding forth a lighted candle, he leads me down a steep circular staircase to a subterranean medieval crypt. Dark shadows silhouette against ancient stone walls as we descend into a dank, musty alcove—the monk's cell beneath the monastery. Candlelight illumines a wooden crucifix that hangs above a bed of straw covering the dirt floor. Making the sign of the Cross, Brother blesses me before leaving.

Alone, I inspect the hovel... Finely spun curtains of silken cobwebs drape everywhere.... Inverted in sleep, bats hang menacingly from the ceiling.... Half-hidden in the shadows of a stony crevice a rat watches; his beady eyes glisten ominously in the candle's muted yellow light. Ignoring his presence, I lay down on the straw. Weary from the day's journey, I fall asleep....

Yeah, right.... Like I'm going to fall asleep in a cave full of spiders, bats and a hungry rat licking his chops at the prospect of dinner—not in *my* life! This medieval fairy tale was written purely for entertainment by a deranged Gothic imagination on steroids; a Stephen King-size whopper of a fictional fabrication, a fib meant to shock your socks off—don't believe a word of it. The gospel truth is: I did sleep in a 12th-century style medieval Norman castle renovated into a monastery, but on a comfortable bed in a room with heat, electricity and indoor plumbing; this lowly hermit had moved uptown to his own bathroom and shower.

I worked in the fields with monks, picking fruit and vegetables: green beans, peas, plums, gooseberries and current berries that the monks would prepare and serve at dinner. Much of our day was spent maintaining the grounds, including the huge apple and plum orchards that lay outside the garden walls. Also weeding, watering and cutting grass in and around one of the largest and oldest walled gardens in Ireland, dating from the 17th century.

Created on the broad slope of a hill, the garden has been terraced and cultivated on four levels, each connected by an ancient stone staircase. Each level of flowers and vegetables is enclosed by a 10-foot tall stone wall partially covered with ivy and other vines. One terrace, called the Bible garden, contains plant species of the Old and New Testament. The fuchsia grows here; with delicately draping flowers this bush thrives throughout Ireland, often creating hedgerows on either side of country lanes. One of the monks explained to me that Irish call the lovely scarlet flowers of the fuchsia "tears of God."

Stones are used to create unique and interesting architectural landscapes such as the walled gardens at Glenstal Abbey. With the island's bumper crop of limestone as plentiful in the fields as buttercups and bog cotton the Irish have had plenty of time and material to hone their stonemasonry skills, and through the centuries have built everything—from walled gardens to churches, castles, cottages, and ever-present dry stone walls. Stones are also featured on a smaller scale to grace cottage gardens. One of the many pleasures of my pilgrimage in Ireland was observing the garden artistry complimenting traditional cottages and modern homes.

The Fathers and Brothers of Glenstal Abbey garden their souls with the same disciplined devotion that they landscape the grounds of the monastery. Following St. Benedict's Rule, the priests and monks celebrate Mass and chant Psalms in Latin. My life as a "monk" consisted of attending Matins at 6:30 a.m.; breakfast of porridge and fruit at 7:30 a.m.; working in the field, with a break for tea at 10:00 a.m. and returning to the field until noon Mass. After a lunch of vegetables and meat or fish I returned to the field to work until 4:00 p.m.; then I would spend the afternoon strolling peaceful monastery grounds or hiking the surrounding hills of County Limerick. Vespers was at 6:30 p.m. and a light dinner at 7:30, with Compline (evening prayers) at 8:30; around 9:30 Father Francis would come to my room to talk with me, read scripture and pray. This was a typical day.

During my stay at the monastery Father Patrick escorted me to a well-secured room beneath the abbey church to view a rare collection of Russian Orthodox ikons. An Irish family who presented them to Glenstal Abbey in the 1950s collected these venerated paintings in France after World War One. Father graciously explained to me the history and religious symbolism of each ikon.

I was blessed with the opportunity to spend time—4 days during the first pilgrimage and 8 days the next summer—experiencing monastic life and developing friendships with the priests and monks who reside at Glenstal Abbey. I wanted to return to the monastery on my second pilgrimage, but decided against, not wanting to impose. However, with the destruction of my tent and with the Euros in my pocket rapidly dwindling I could either sleep under the stars (and rain) or swallow my pride and seek refuge at the monastery. I glanced up at the swollen rain clouds and swallowed my pride.

From experience I have learned that Divine Providence sometimes works in mysterious ways; the destruction of my tent, I truly believe, was the Lord's way of persuading this proud 12th-century medieval hermit to humbly return to his roots. Of course, Father Patrick and the folks at the Abbey warmly welcomed this pilgrim, graciously providing food and shelter to a homeless wanderer. Once again I was to experience that His way, mysterious or not, works.

At the end of my second pilgrimage to Glenstal Abbey, the Fathers and Brothers of the monastery insisted on purchasing a train ticket for me so that when time came to fly back to the States I could spend my last day in Dublin rather than on the road hitchhiking. I spent much of that day at Dublin Castle visiting Christ Church Cathedral and Chester Beatty Library with its collection of art, literary manuscripts and priceless fragments of New Testament Scripture dating back to 200 A.D.

As attested by this incredible library, Christianity has a well-documented historical "paper trail" that clearly refutes the misguided idea that the basic tenets of Christian theology are mythology that has evolved over time. Anyone—especially we who are Protestant—would do well to read the early Church Fathers of Roman Catholic and Eastern Orthodox spirituality: Sts. Augustine, Chrysostom, Basil and countless others who, through their lives and written words, are a great cloud of witnesses to the historicity of the Christian faith. We Protestants sometimes dismiss the Church of the dark and medieval centuries as an institution fraught with ignorance and superstition. By doing this we *in our ignorance* forfeit much of our wonderful Christian heritage.

Many people do not appreciate the debt civilization owes the early Catholic monks of Ireland. When barbarian tribes from northern Europe were plundering the Roman Empire, monks in "beehive" cells in Ireland were copying the classical and religious literature of Western Civilization, the foundation of our dearest held values and institutions. These books would have been lost forever to history except for the work of these monks.

While on the subject of literati of Western civilization, did I mention that I am a poet? That is, I call myself a poet; I've learned from experience that one can call oneself anything one pleases. I could call myself a rocket scientist, or brain surgeon, or nuclear physicist, or computer engineer. However, being an unassuming 12th-century medieval hermit, I prefer the lower profile, unpretentious title of "poet" as a way to ingratiate myself into the exclusive fraternity of Homer, Dante, Chaucer, Shakespeare, William Wordsworth and, of course, Walt Whitman—this prestige without having to take the tough math and science courses those other titles require. Smart thinking, don't you think? I graduated college using this kind of logic!

To provide at least a façade of legitimacy to this title I even wrote some poetry and generously offered my work to publishers. Editors, scribbling on rejection slips, had the temerity to return my verse, affixed with unsolicited and, shall I say, less than ingratiating critiques of my poems (the audacity of these pretentious snobs)! Like Biblical prophets of old, this poet was without honor in his own country. So, not finding an appreciative audience in America, I packed my grip and in a snit, left for Ireland to self-publish in the land of poets by handing my verse to folk on streets, in pubs, in the hinterlands, wherever people were to be found....

This hermit was on a mission, hoofing and thumbing through the Emerald Isle, giving copies of poetry to people everywhere: drivers who stopped for this road-weary hitchhiker; farmers who permitted this roving gypsy to pitch his tent; proprietors of hotels, hostels and B&Bs who provided bathing facilities to this unwashed vagabond;

pub tenders and patrons full of blarney, music and sometimes, sage advice; the priests and monks who twice welcomed this wayfaring stranger with hot meals and a comfortable bed; people, whatever their station and circumstance, who provided kind Irish hospitality to this lowly 12th-century medieval hermit.

Dear reader, having squandered in riotous monastery living the few remaining Euros in my pocket, our pilgrimage of Ireland has come to an abrupt bankrupt end. (So be it, I have nothing more to write worth reading anyway.) Unlike the prodigal son who returned to his forgiving father to live a respectable life of sobriety, this prodigal husband returned to his long-suffering wife to begin a scam career as travel writer, with the inebriated pipe dream of recouping some of that squandered loot; hence the book you are holding in your hand.

How well have I succeeded in this nefarious enterprise? Please indulge me as I take an informal reader survey: Have you wasted your money in purchasing this book? If you think not, thank you, I smell success! If you think so, you are obviously an astute reader who is not duped by mindless drivel—this book was not meant for you. However, with exaggerated conscience of creeping old age, I feel your pain and will try to make amends by generously throwing into the kitty the remainder of my poetry that I was unable to sneak into the text. Does this self-promoting display of hubris sweeten the deal? No? OK, but before you consult legal counsel please lend a commiserating ear as I spin my tragic story. Bear with me; this is pretty emotional; it won't be easy.

Hidden in the creepy-crawly cellar of what once was an uncorrupted youthful heart lurks the dark side of my rapidly balding hermit nature, albeit kept shackled in a fiery pit, never to be trotted out into the light of day for public scrutiny. We all have our demons, do we not? In this perennially crowded field of *wood-be* personal demons, the odds-on people's choice for this or any other year *wood be* demon rum, *wood it* not? *Wood* that my *wood-be* demon *wood be* demon rum—that *wood-be* demon *woodn't be* worth his horns to this *wood-be* tea-totler, *wood it*? Knock on would!

My private demon is popular—but not *that* popular! My demon is mammon, AKA filthy lucre, translate, cash money—or to get to the root of the evil, the *love* of money; and rooting even deeper in this cesspool, the love of *your* money!!! That's right, this all too human dark side of me, tempted by the lure of your wallet, is up to my neck as I root through muck and mire in quest of fool's gold.

Shameful? Absolutely! Successful? The jury's still out, so I'll continue to root—up to my eyeballs now—for the love of money. The rims of my glasses and then my receding hairline are swallowed by the muck. Soon all that remain above the mire, like a white flag hoisted in surrender, are a few feathery sprigs of thinning gray hair. Air bubbles ominously rise to the surface even as the jury foreman rises to his feet to announce the verdict. This fraudulent 12th-century medieval hermit looks at the mirror to see an unshaven, aging face of guilt staring back—trust me, it *ain't* a pretty sight! I wrote this essay not with the noble purpose of educating, enlightening, edifying and uplifting you, dear reader. This tawdry rag of socially unredeemable tabloid journalism was written as a hook baited with the tempting and intentionally come-hither cover title of *Ireland on $10 a Day* to catch suckers like you; but with poor sales, the plot has been foiled. The moral to this story: crime doesn't pay union scale; in fact, it doesn't pay enough for a fellow to make an *honest* living. Never has and never will!

I have succumbed to my inner beast. By placing my hope for a solvent financial future not where it should be, in heavenly wisdom from above, but in the jaded ethics of yellow journalism, I have been tried in the court of public opinion by a jury of my peers—as fate would have it, you, dear readers. And no surprise here, you found me guilty as charged, condemning this hermit to the gallows of his conscience.... Waiting on death row with (excuse the pun) time to kill, I ask myself: self, what is the ethic of the marketplace that will condemn a pitiful street waif, orphaned at birth and abandoned on the steps of the almshouse, to a childhood of peddling newspapers on snowy sidewalks for his bowl of porridge; then, in a mere 50 years, turn him into a cranky sociopath hack writer of mindless drivel, albeit drivel that will sell like hotcakes someday, fingers crossed, to become a runaway bestseller, topping the *New York Times* bestseller list and catapulting its arrogant, vainglorious author to guest appearances on *Late Show with David Letterman*, *The Tonight Show with Jay Leno* and *World Wrestling Federation*; even as I search my soul for that youthful street corner newsboy with his honest work ethic, I find instead a conniving 12th-century medieval hermit gone bad, and so I plead with you, if only for the sake of that pure and innocent street waif, to search the ugly quagmire of this heinously convoluted run-on sentence for that sweet kid gone missing, and while you're at it, keep an eye open for that flirtatious donkey gone sour? The last sentence did begin, once upon a time, as a question, didn't it? This was *my* childhood (albeit revised and edited by my guilt-ridden attorney as a last-ditch effort to affect a stay of execution at least until my check clears the bank). Be merciful to this poor abandoned orphan.

In my personal tragedy there is a lesson for you, dear reader! What malevolent spirit can magically create a demand for all manner of unwanted, unneeded and highly dubious goods and services—products that didn't exist last week, but this week suddenly become, along with oxygen, the very necessities of life and are hawked like hotcakes on eBay and the Home Shopping Network? What is the name of this devil that dwells in the darkest cellar of the soul, enabler of shopping malls, flea markets, insurance salesmen and rogue hucksters like me? Dear reader, the name of this demon is *human gullibility*—that most abundant and ever-renewable diabolic resource; the power that drives you, against your better judgment, to fork over hard earned cash to a variety of shysters, con artists, scallywags, TV preachers, and hack writers of cheap paperbacks. You can't deny this: the evidence is in your hands even as you read these carefully baited words. Lest you fall prey to the next scam, please heed the eloquent words of that great American sideshow carnie barker—*slash*—cynic philosopher, P.T. Barnum: *"There's a sucker born every minute!"*

Not conceived in conventional horizontal hula fashion, but creatively molded from a mud ball, Adam soon lost a rib, but gained a wife, Eve (the wisdom of this trade is still being hotly debated around office water coolers). Together they became the prototypes for a whole world of suckers to come. On self-serving advice of a forked-tongued, glib talking realtor, these two love-smitten honeymooners sold their perfectly comfortable home (a wedding gift from their father) for an apple and a promise of "knowledge!" What was this dearly purchased knowledge? *"Never give a sucker an even chance!"* This was no garden variety con job, but was the Louisiana Purchase of real-estate scams, setting the "sucker" standard for nearly six millenniums, only surpassed in the 6th decade of the 20th century when the Chicago Cubs traded Lou Brock to the St. Louis Cardinals for Ernie Broglio. *Ernie who???....* SUCKERS!!!

In the yin-yang circle of life, what goes around comes around. And for me what came around was the stench of bad karma from hustling in a cesspool of avarice! Pride goes before the fall: In my greed for your money I unwittingly cast myself in the role of "sucker" in my own stage play, proudly exalting in my stealth as this whirling dervish wordsmith baited the hook, *Ireland on $10 a Day*, and went a' fishing for suckers. Spoiled by easy monastery living, this 12th-century medieval hermit lost his appetite for stale bread and was no longer content sleeping in pastures with sheep, he lusted for the night life—the pub life with its Irish stew, Guinness and fiddle music. Even as he fished for suckers to finance a night on the town, this backsliding hermit scripted his own doom by staying in character to the bitter end of the soap opera. A funny thing happened on the way to the pub: I caught the biggest sucker of all—myself—and received the wages of sin, going belly up in that cesspool of muck and mire, proving once again that *there's a sucker born every minute*!

Some Forgotten Character

On some secluded park bench
Fading to December gray
Some forgotten character
From some forgotten play
Keeps his lonely vigil
As he does most every day
Of children in the park
Laughing as they play....
He thinks of summer rainbows
This bleak December day
Arching round the world
Promising tomorrow
To children as they play....
He listens to their laughter
Near the end of day
Finding comfort in their joy
As stage lights fade away
And final curtains fall
On some forgotten character
From some forgotten play.

EXCUSE ME WHILE I HIGHTAIL TO the last refuge of a scoundrel: May I, as one Christian to another, ask your gracious forgiveness? And while I have you in a forgiving mood, will you accept in lieu of any court-ordered financial settlement, the rest of my poetry as restitution in full. Sign on the dotted line, please. Bless you!

Before I pony up the remainder of my verse to close this sale, I will present my hiking orders (made all the more poignant as I open my mail to a final eviction notice). Excerpted from the autobiography of an anonymous 19th-century Russian hermit on pilgrimage to Jerusalem, entitled *The Way of a Pilgrim*: By The Grace Of God I am a Christian man, by my own actions a great sinner, and by calling a homeless wanderer of the humblest origins, roaming from place to place. My worldly belongings consist of a knapsack on my back, containing some dried bread, and a Holy Bible in my breast pocket. That is all....

Sailors of Eternity

O' Sloop Humanity,
We sailors of Eternity,
Behold the Rock
Ever standing watch
Beside the raging sea....
Beware!
The blackest night would blind our sight
But for this Beacon's guiding light,
So setting sail unto home port
Seek harbor in His love;
Take courage, sailors,
Behold our Lord!
He guides us from above.

His Lovely Garden Place

A universe of lifeless space
Surrounds His lovely garden place
Where trellised vines
Of honeysuckle's verdant hue
Hide robin's nest of eggs sky blue
With sunshine splicing sudden showers
Splashing blooms of rainbow flowers:
Morning glories,
Daffodils,
Tulips too
With Easter lilies,
Like our Savior,
Tried and true.
In His lovely garden place
As we slept Jesus prayed,
"Father, take this burden
From Your Son
Though not my will
But yours be done."
Then with a kiss betrayed,
Mocked and spat on,
Scourged, despised,
Nailed to a cross
Christ crucified.
"Forgive them, Father,
For they know
Not what they do,"
Speaks our Savior,
Tried and true.

DON CARMICHAEL

Two thousand years
Yet eyes of faith
Still look beyond
A universe of lifeless space
To our Risen, Living Lord:
Eternal God's Easter Gift
Of Saving Grace
To fallen children
Of His lovely garden place.

Cathedral Bells

Cathedral bells sounding
Summon faithful from their toil,
The peasant in the field
Leaves his sickle with the soil,
The maiden in the cottage
Sets her broom aside
As they hasten to the chapel
To Christ the Crucified;
Cathedral bells calling
To worship and to prayer
The weaver and the potter,
The miller and the mayor,
Christians of our village
We meet in one accord
Gathered in the chapel
To praise our Risen Lord.

COPIES OF THE PRECEDING THREE POEMS were given to folk I met along the way in Ireland, with my silent prayers of blessings to its readers. The following verse is offered to you, my fellow pilgrims, in appreciation of your fortitude in sticking with me to the bitter end of this pilgrimage in prose and poetry.... You have earned your stripes; sew them to your hermit's tunic—and wear them proudly!

Yesterday, Today, Tomorrow...

*Forever is a long, long time
Conveniently divided
By calendars of months and weeks
With every day decided,
No time to lend or borrow:
As yesterday, so today
And surely so tomorrow....
Life is neither very long
Nor easily divided
By calendars fortuitous
With fate to be decided,
Time strewn with joy and sorrow:
As yesterday, so today
And surely so tomorrow....*

Cost of Living

The marketplace
Though difficult to understand
Determines cost of living:
Buying versus selling,
Supply against demand;
The human heart
A marketplace
No less to comprehend:
Cost of living is in giving,
Caring and in sharing,
With currency of love to spend.

Silence Speaks

Across the street from Forest Park
In an affluent St. Louis neighborhood
Of stately old homes an elderly gentleman
Tends his rose garden.
As I watch,
Our eyes meet,
And with the moment
Strangers speak
Across the lawn.
Later, in the primate house of the park zoo
An African gorilla chews pieces of straw.
The animal seems to exude quiet dignity
Not unlike the gentleman
Tending roses.
As I watch,
Our eyes meet,
And with the moment
Silence speaks
Across eternity.

Sheltered

Sheltered in her father's arms
She peeks into the evening sky
To wonder of a moon not round,
"Daddy, tell me why?"
A less than perfect moon above
This less than perfect world below,
He thinks but does not say
knowing she will learn someday...
Need be her private way.

Simple Little Things

Grandpa built a cupboard
With pine he cut himself,
And grandma with her loving touch
Placed on every shelf
Those simple little things of life
That never seem like much—
Salt and pepper shakers,
Cups and saucers too—
Her cupboard filled with such:
Those simple little things of life
That grandma loved so much.

Walking in the Woods

While walking in the woods today
I find a friend along the way;
Into the tangled ivy
She has fallen from her nest—
My fragile little friend,
Please Lord, let her rest.
I cup her in my palm
As I place her in the nest—
My precious little friend,
Our prayers are truly blest!

Autumn Beauty

Countless crimson ballerinas dancing down the Maple tree
Beneath October's sunny blue umbrella canopy;
The artist's palette can but capture thee
While the poet muses pensively:
Why this leaf-strewn ballet fantasy
When much too brief her scarlet blushing spree
And far too fair for art or verse to mimic thee!
Artists, poets hearken unto nature's plea:
Why fall prey to jealousy
When autumn beauty is meant to be—
Not to tease thy artistry,
Nor reprove thy poetry—
Just to bless and humble thee!

My Pilgrim Friend

Springs of life-sustaining waters
Well from living stones,
Spilling over pastures
To meander grassy meadows
And wander walnut groves;
This spry old prairie pilgrim
Hiking ancient stony paths
Brings cups of living water
To multitudes of children
Our mother nature has:
Bless'ed brother Robin,
Saintly sister Rose;
Beside this faithful brook
Our prairie family grows....
Saturday shall find me
Rising with the sun,
Rucksack over shoulder,
A precious day to spend
In prairie fields a' hiking
With my pilgrim friend;
I tell him of my troubles,
He in his quiet way
Gently reassures
And helps me understand:
With life there is meaning,
A purpose and a plan.

Having returned to my home, the United States of America, I am often asked if I will pull my donkey cart through Ireland again. My answer: I don't know what the future holds. I would like to return to Ireland some day, but no matter; there will always be a place in my heart for this lovely island and her people. All I know for sure is that this old donkey will pull his cart of worn-out flesh and bones to his grave, but no farther! Then I will cross over to the other side, into a timeless Eternity where, by way of comparison, even the earthly beauty of the Emerald Isle will fade to nothing.